Introduction

In the fall of 2006, we both enrolled as students in the School of Intercultural Studies at Fuller Theological Seminary (Pasadena, Calif.). We were drawn to southern California by the prospect of studying the field of missiology and for the opportunity to learn from and engage urban, multicultural expressions of Anabaptism. Moreover, southern California seemed to offer an ideal context for exploring questions about Anabaptism in a "post-this, post-that" cultural context and to gain insight into the realities confronting the church in the 21st century.

As students of missiology we have spent considerable time learning about the significant historical, theological and cultural transformations the Christian church is experiencing. Over the course of the past century, Christianity has truly become a global religion with Latin America, Africa and Asia emerging as the new centers and expressions of the faith. The current experience within the Anabaptist family has been no exception. Indeed, what is happening in southern California is an expression of a trend reflected worldwide, making it a microcosm of the global macrocosmic reality.

An important part of our seminary experience has been the relationships we have built with fellow brothers and sisters in Christ, relationships that have challenged our thinking, affirmed our gifts, supported and nurtured us, and given us new ways of looking at the world. These relationships have taught us to recognize that:

- The Christian family is a diverse one because the Christian faith always finds expression in particular, local forms.
- The church must engage its own culture in intentional, missional ways if it expects to witness to it.

- It is mission, more than anything else, that provides meaning and purpose to a church struggling with its identity.
- Sixteenth-century Anabaptist issues need to be translated into 21st-century, multicultural realities.
- Voices of renewal within the church often come from those on the margins.

The following essays were inspired by a gathering of the Anabaptist Association of Missiologists (AAM) held several years ago in Pasadena. Consultation participants sought to explore the theme, "Whose Anabaptist Vision? Implications for Mission from a Southern California Perspective," by examining the uniqueness and relevancy of historic Anabaptism in this locale, as well as Anabaptism in its newer forms and expressions currently being shaped by evangelical, emergent, immigrant and multicultural realities.

The essays found here, therefore, constitute a set of views and voices that provide a glimpse into the emerging contours of Anabaptism, informing our perspectives regarding its embodiment today. We hope that these reflections communicate a sense of "place" by providing a snapshot of faith lived out in the context of 21st-century southern California.

Matthew Krabill and David Stutzman, editors

Forward

The actual practice of Christian faith is a journey lived in the balance between a transcultural global expression of God's redemptive intent, and a grounded, local incarnation of God's redemptive action. Said another way, Jesus Christ is the same yesterday, today and forever, and the good news of Jesus Christ is yet somehow different in every locale.

The essays presented here tell a bit of the story of the good news as experienced by Anabaptists in southern California. These Anabaptists are not those of Schleitheim, Goshen, Molotschna or Newton. These Anabaptists practice their faith along freeway snarls and urban sprawl, during drought and earthquakes, and often with uncertain immigration status.

Their reflections remind us that place matters. The geography of souls takes shape in a concrete, historical context. A specific environment forms the contours of faith. Following Christ daily in Los Angeles presents different challenges and requires different responses than following Christ daily in Lancaster, Pa. This truth invites us to both deeper reflection and joyful celebration.

The above assertion is not mere relativism. Paying attention to place as the crucible of Christian discipleship reminds us that all ideologies, including our theologies, are provisional. The first-century affirmation of faith was one simple sentence: "Jesus is Lord." Neither historical creeds nor denominational statements speak equally as well. In every environment, ideology tends to lack incarnational reality. The essays in these pages invite us to consider the possibility that our location affects our salvation. Our salvation, our redemption, and God's missional purposes continue to draw us forward into God's grand, eternal scheme of things, but the ways and means in which we discover and experience the grace of God through Christ are most certainly shaped by our geography. Place matters.

In southern California, place is an expression of what missiologists call "liminality." Southern California is a borderland between nations, languages, races and classes. The rich and poor stand cheek and jowl next to every tongue and tribe and language and culture.

In some other places where Anabaptists have lived, place conspired with history and served to create at least the illusion of a faith-based fortress from the world. My wife grew up in the wheat and cattle country of northwestern Oklahoma in a small, low-German-speaking hamlet of security called Kremlin—the Russian word for "fortress."

The Anabaptist experience in southern California is different by the very inability of the community to garrison itself off in a Mennonite colony. Despite occasional attempts to replicate this experience of Mennonites in other parts of the country, the simple reality is that the spiritual, social and economic geography of this place makes the formation of Mennonite cultural enclaves very difficult to sustain.

The following essays invite us to consider the richness of diverse Anabaptist experiences; they cause us to wrestle with what is truly at the core of our faith. They ask us: Does being Anabaptist require of us a strong boundary of similar practices, similar institutions, and similar safeguards? Can we be Anabaptist by committing to a simple core of mutual obligations, practiced in a diversity of ways? How much stress can our need for a defined edge hold? How little actually needs to be in the center of our faith and praxis for there to be real unity and common identity?

It is my hope that the pages to follow will inspire and confound readers in a quest to engage these and related questions. Place does indeed matter. Let's explore what that means for us ... together.

Jeff Wright

Jeff Wright has lived in southern California since 1986 and now resides in Riverside, Calif. He served as executive director of the Center for Anabaptist Leadership (1992-2009) and as a conference minister in the Pacific Southwest Mennonite Conference (1996-2009). Wright is pastor of the Madison Street Church and executive director of the Madison Street Community Development Ministry. He also serves as principal consultant for Urban Expression North America, a church-planting consultancy that currently serves the Eastern District and Atlantic Coast Conferences of Mennonite Church USA.

New Anabaptist Voices

Matthew Krabill and David Stutzman, editors

Anabaptist values are "good news" for displaced immigrants

Hyun and Sue Hur

A day in the worship life of our community

10:30 a.m.

It's Sunday morning, and the smell of dark French roast coffee fills our small house. The television is rolled into our kids' room, and the living room has been vacuumed by our son 30 minutes ago. Our neighbor, Pablo Kim, knocks on the door with a pink box stuffed with donuts from down the street. Slowly, people trickle into the kitchen greeting us

Sue and Hyun Hur

with *"annyung-hasae-yo," "hola"* and "hello" as they grab their morning coffee, milk and donuts. They return to the living room and read together a couple of chapters from Matthew before the service starts.

11 a.m.

Worship begins, but not always on time. Since there are only about six families, we usually wait until everyone arrives. Hyun and Daniel grab their guitars to begin worship. The praise songs are sung in English in the beginning since the majority of the children in our church cannot read Korean. After the children are blessed and dismissed, the message is shared in Korean followed by a time of sharing and prayer in small groups.

12:30 p.m.

The children return from Pablo's house, located next door. They have just finished rehearsing a drama script about the work of the Holy Spirit from *Gather 'Round*[1] which they will present to the adults next week. We sing our "sending song" together, take communion with naan bread and grape juice, and "pass the peace" with each member present.

1 p.m.

It's lunch time, so we head over to Daniel and Sara's house, adjacent to ours. We share a common meal together in the living room with the adults huddling around the large coffee table and the children gathering around the foldable Korean table. For some of us Americanized ones who have difficulty sitting on the floor for long periods of time, we sit by the dining table in the kitchen.

3 p.m.

We invite two of our regular attendees back to our house to have an introductory Bible study in Korean. This is the first time that the two have ever studied the Bible regularly. One of them is already asking how he can be baptized. Another group meets for a short Bible study session to discuss *What Is an Anabaptist Christian?*—a publication of Mennonite Mission Network in their *Missio Dei* series.[2] During this time, several of the men who work on Saturdays head to Pablo's house to nap, and several of the women gather to work on their latest quilting project.

5:30 p.m.

Daniel and Sara's house is full of activity again as we prepare for dinner. Today's menu is homemade noodles with seafood broth. As an experienced cook, Jason kneads and begins to roll out the dough. The children gather excitedly around the kitchen table to see the chef at work.

8 p.m.

It is time to go home. The children moan wanting to stay a little longer. The rest of the church members slowly gather their belongings and head

---

[1] Bible-based curriculum for children, youth and their families developed by Mennonite and Church of the Brethren publishers (see www.gatherround.org).
[2] See this issue and others in the series at www.MennoniteMission.net/Resources/MissioDei/Pages/Home.aspx.

to their cars. Hugs and waves are exchanged before heading back to Diamond Bar, Koreatown, Burbank and Anaheim (Calif.).

Why Anabaptism?

We are not sure if this snapshot of one of our typical Sundays depicts the experiences of other small Anabaptist house churches. However, the reason that we began this church plant in the first place stems from our desire to have our church core values and beliefs be clearly Anabaptist.

Being one of the only Korean Mennonite churches in the United States, we are often asked the question why we chose to become Anabaptists. In spite of the dynamic achievements made by the Korean church in the homeland and in many international settings, there are serious challenges facing the future of this church that must be thoughtfully addressed. Among them are issues of nominalism, individualism, and conflict resolution.

The Anabaptist Vision states the essence of faith as discipleship, the essence of the church as community, and the essence of ethics as love and nonresistance.

The search for biblical answers to these concerns drew us to the Anabaptists. We have explored the confession of Anabaptism encapsulated by Harold S. Bender in *The Anabaptist Vision* that states the essence of faith as discipleship, the essence of the church as community, and the essence of ethics as love and nonresistance.[3] Moreover, Anabaptists have 500 years of rich history that testify to their faith practiced in everyday life. We strongly believe that the Anabaptist confession and history offer a tangible model that can greatly influence today's Korean church to engage in significant questions and insights toward renewal and mission. With the conviction that Anabaptism can create a deeper and richer dialogue among Korean Christians, we have decided to become Anabaptists.

Immigrant context

Our desire is to live out the Anabaptist vision of discipleship, community and peacemaking in our immigrant church context. And we believe that these core values can best be expressed in our missional context through the practice of hospitality as a community. We find commonality with early Anabaptists who sought refuge from persecution and who cared

---

[3] Harold Bender, *The Anabaptist Vision* (Scottdale, PA: Herald Press, 1944).

for families of martyrs.[4] Because they faced severe persecution and were displaced from their homes, Anabaptists had to depend on other members of their faith community and the hospitality of their neighbors to survive. In this way, they grew to value the practice of hospitality as a necessary way of life.

Although immigrants in the United States don't experience persecution in quite the same way as the early Anabaptists, we can identify with the struggle of displacement and the need to depend on the hospitality of neighbors to survive in the immigrant experience. Many immigrants feel isolated being away from their families and home countries and placed in a foreign country with a new language and way of life. Those who do have families in the United States often have difficulty with their marriages from the stress of surviving from one paycheck to the next. Some who have become illegal residents when their student visa process did not come through, feel utterly lost in a country that has not welcomed them. For these people, there is a deep need to feel safe and recognize that they are heard, known and loved.

> We can identify with the struggle of displacement and the need to depend on the hospitality of neighbors to survive in the immigrant experience.

We are discovering that the best way to show that these people are part of a community that embraces them is to live in community. Recently, God began to open up opportunities for several members of our church families to move close to our house to begin an intentional community. Throughout the week, many of our church members stop by to eat, learn English, quilt, garden, rest, seek counsel, or study with other members of our emerging community. As we practice and observe the power of hospitality, we see that the spirit of Anabaptism flows through us.

Hyun Hur pastors a Korean Mennonite church called Church for Others in Temple City, Calif., and serves as a board member of Pacific Southwest Mennonite Conference. In his spare time, Hyun enjoys reading and learning how to free-dive with church members. Sue works as a director of Language Transit, an after-school academy in Arcadia. Together, they have three children, Guhn (11), Lynn (9) and Yul (1).

---

[4] Christine Pohl, *Making Room* (Grand Rapids, MI: Eerdmans Publishing Company, 1999).

The creative alternative many Christians are looking for

Tommy Airey

Tommy
Airey

In my part of the world, Orange County (OC), Calif., Anabaptists are about as rare as snowstorms. South OC, where my wife and I live and work, represents some of the wealthiest neighborhoods in the state, even the nation. The median home price after several years of recession and falling prices is still around $500,000. Everything from lawns to people is well-manicured. The OC offers a smorgasbord of evangelical mega-churches, malls and vacation resorts.

In the fall of 2005, my wife and I started fighting the traffic to get to Fuller Seminary in Pasadena. We were jaded with the conservative evangelicalism we had grown up in. And we were brimming with questions about the Bible, the gospel, church, evangelism, and the role of faith and politics.

At the beginning of our seminary journey, we had no idea what "Anabaptism" meant, but soon we were taking classes with Erin Dufault-Hunter, Nancey Murphy, Wilbert Shenk and David Augsburger, as well as reading the likes of John Howard Yoder, James McClendon and Glen Stassen. We became hooked on the disciple-making, simple-living, peace-loving, revolutionary-subordinating radical reformers. Through our studies, conversations and brief experiences, we came to see this "minority report" of the body of Christ as the most compelling brand of Christian faith available.

Four key factors pulling us toward Anabaptism

There have been some key factors that impacted our magnetic pull toward Anabaptism.

- **First,** the shallowness of the conservative evangelical gospel, often limited to personal piety and eternal salvation in heaven, has been challenged and enhanced by the Anabaptist depth of discipleship and salvation as a way of life.
- **Second,** the *cross* had always been narrowly defined as Jesus dying in the place of *my* sins so that *I* could go to heaven when *I* die. But the Anabaptists have taught us to take up the cross of Jesus' powerful confrontation with the powers-that-be, with the consequent challenge that entails for social nonconformity in 21st-century America.

- **Third,** the kingdom of God is no longer only an inner and future reality. It is, instead, the primary allegiance for disciples *now* and at every level of our existence—personal, social, economic and political.
- **Fourth,** the hierarchical CEO leadership model of most churches has been debunked by the Anabaptist notion that all of God's children are called to mission and ministry at the moment of their freely-chosen baptism. Jesus' definition of leadership, we have learned, demands a more humble, service-oriented stance where all in the faith community are leaders, whether seminary trained or not.

> Through our studies, conversations and brief experiences, we came to see this "minority report" of the body of Christ as the most compelling brand of Christian faith available.

In the past few years, my wife and I have had the privilege of hosting and facilitating two Anabaptist-style house-church communities where we've emphasized these theological strands. In reality, these gatherings were glorified "young adult Bible studies" for Christian disciples who had become jaded by their OC evangelical experience. Of the two dozen folks who participated in these communities, perhaps one-fourth would today claim the title "Anabaptist." We have used the title sparingly, but have tried to model the Anabaptist way during our meetings and, more importantly, though imperfectly, with our lifestyle.

The importance of Anabaptism in today's culture

I have come to believe that Anabaptism, in our current cultural milieu, is intensely relevant for a number of reasons.

- **First** of all, there are widespread sensibilities among younger Christians in their 20s and 30s that our collective American response to the tragedy of 9/11 has faltered. Our impulse for revenge and the resulting wars have not only cost taxpayers trillions of dollars and led to more animosity from the world community, but they also cannot be supported by God's word. Reading the New Testament through the Anabaptist lens of peace, enemy love, and reconciliation illuminates the unique and radical Christian nonviolent vocation in this historic moment of time. More and more in the decades to come, Americans will recognize the foolishness of our wayward mentality.
- **Second,** since December 2007, the economic recession has uncovered the greed and materialism of both Wall Street and Main Street. We are all implicated in a way of life that is unsustainable. Many of us have

made economic decisions beyond our means as banks have targeted the vulnerable and become wealthier following the government's bailout. For Anabaptists, the gospel calls us to live simply in order to share abundantly, while advocating for the victims of predatory lending. We can be "set apart" during this harsh time of unemployment and economic restructuring by being a people who transcend the economic schizophrenia of spending and hoarding.

- **Third,** there has been a backlash from many non-Christian Americans because of the political marriage between evangelicals and the Republican party. It has had the unintended consequence of defining what a Christian is in the United States—someone who fights against abortion, gay marriage and terrorism, while embracing free-market principles and American patriotism, all in God's name. Anabaptist ecclesiology emphasizes the community's primary allegiance to the multinational reign of God—a radical, compelling way of life.
- **Last,** because Anabaptist communities have often lived in marginalized settings, they have an ingrained ethos of humility, service and compassion that contrasts with the triumphalistic, colonizing tone and approach of much of the American church in the past 300 years. A Christian community who listens to "the other" and models an alternative way of life will gather a hearing in a world longing for the fulfillment, joy, love and healing that only the gospel can bring.

> I truly believe that Anabaptism is the "missing link" for Christian disciples in Orange County and in American society more broadly...

Anabaptism offers American Christians a creative alternative

In the United States, we continue to live in an Enlightenment hangover that offers Protestant Christians roughly two choices, mainline liberal and conservative evangelical. Many Christians have settled into one of these two streams. But increasingly, growing numbers of people are repelled by these two options and either are bailing out on Christian faith altogether or are boldly seeking creative alternatives. As I wrestle with what it means to be Christian in our context, I truly believe that Anabaptism is the "missing link" for Christian disciples in Orange County and in American society more broadly—disciples who are longing for a richer, more compelling Christian faith in light of the baggage American Christianity and culture have to offer.

Tommy Airey teaches high-school government and economics. He and his wife, Lindsay, discovered Anabaptism when they studied at Fuller Seminary, graduating with degrees in Theology and in Marriage and Family Therapy, respectively. They currently live in Irvine, Calif., and host a small church community in their studio apartment every Sunday morning. In addition, Tommy runs marathons, co-directs the "Anabaptist Network in North America," and blogs at www.easyyolk.blogspot.com.

Extending to fellow Christians an invitation to the Anabaptist stream of God's story
Erin Dufault-Hunter

Erin
Dufault-
Hunter

Not long ago, I sat in a faculty meeting at Fuller Theological Seminary to debate whether we as a seminary should affirm a collaborative program with the U.S. Air Force chaplaincy. A number of faculty were deeply disturbed by such a proposal on several grounds, from Christian pacifism to more specific concerns about linking our program to one over which we had little control. Those reluctant to affirm this collaborative effort were passionate. As one of the few Anabaptists in the crowd at this interdenominational evangelical seminary, I was pleased with the protests and began to hope it would be defeated. However, when the vote was taken, there was no need to count them. It wasn't even close. The program easily passed with an overwhelming majority.

I was again astounded and disheartened at the different assumptions my brothers and sisters make about what the gospel entails, about what the cross and resurrection at the center of our evangelical faith could possibly mean if we affirm partnership with nationalism, murder and destruction on a massive scale. It is sometimes lonely here, an Anabaptist at sea in a community whose sensibility runs counter to that of my adopted Mennonite faith.

Part of why this remains puzzling and disheartening to me is because of my own encounters with the Gospels, particularly through the Gospel of Mark, and with a Christ who offered me life if I would lose my life, who commanded my allegiance so that I might enjoy true joy.

As an Anabaptist in an evangelical context, I am left with several questions: Why remain in an environment in which the Air Force can be seen as a partner in ministry? How do we witness to our Anabaptist convictions in interdenominational settings? How do we Anabaptists understand our larger mission to the world?

My journey toward Anabaptism

Through the study of scriptures with a group of fellow seekers during my college years, I came to understand that the Sermon on the Mount was not some kind of isolated, radical text, but rather simply *another* text that clarified and confirmed what I increasingly saw as a consistent ethical vision throughout scripture, particularly in the New Testament. Our study group labored for a while under the illusion that *we* had recovered this message of personal salvation with political implications—simplicity, cruciform love even for enemies, and nonviolent resistance to evil in pursuit of God's just peace among them. But fairly soon, we recognized that such sensibility ran throughout the Christian tradition and was most clearly identified with Anabaptist traditions and the Radical Reformation. It was in some ways a blow to our pride, but also deeply reassuring to discover that we were part of the Spirit's ongoing work of calling and shaping disciples.

> …my primary allegiance is never to being an Anabaptist or a pacifist, but to the Lord and Savior we Christians worship.

This experience and others eventually led me and my husband to join a Mennonite church and to commit to a community that holds me accountable to practice what I proclaim, and shapes my habits so that I might one day be the follower of Jesus I desire to become. Without such a community, I too easily lose my way. In community, I am fed by the living witness of those who in large and small ways trust in the hard reality of God's-kingdom-come-near, and who hope for what is yet often unseen.

While I need my local congregation to remind me of my commitments and to sustain me in my values as a Mennonite, I am also grateful to the broader community of Christians in the seminary context who allow me to share widely and deeply in their lives, not only in our intellectual life as students or colleagues, but more importantly as fellow travelers along the way. These friends, too, sustain me in my Christian discipleship, reminding me that the Spirit works in the world not only among "my" people, but all peoples. In an interdenominational setting like Fuller, I and other Anabaptists are often confronted in our convictions. Consequently, this constant rubbing against different interpretations of our Christian history, mission and faith has sharpened my Anabaptist convictions, and reminds me that my primary allegiance is never to being an Anabaptist or a pacifist, but to the Lord and Savior we Christians worship.

Anabaptists need to stay in conversation with fellow Christians

We are called to be witnesses to what God has done, is doing, and will do in Christ. Anabaptists have understood this witness to be as a minority people, never expecting that everyone will agree with us. Yet many people today are hungry for what the Anabaptist tradition offers, not least among them fellow Christians weary of an anemic faith that merely affirms U.S. culture and values. If we isolate ourselves from other Christians who share our allegiance to Jesus, if we shun those who are our natural allies, we cannot extend the invitation into this particular strain of God's story.

> …many people today are hungry for what the Anabaptist tradition offers, not least among them fellow Christians weary of an anemic faith that merely affirms U.S. culture and values.

Menno Simons and our Anabaptist fore-parents used the word "evangelical" in its best sense, as the good news of the kingdom come and coming. We must reclaim this word again, cajoling and wooing our brothers and sisters with whom we share it to consider Jesus anew. Even if they are not fully persuaded, my passion is to move people a bit closer to the truth as expressed in the Anabaptist telling of the story of God in Christ.

One way of describing my life as an Anabaptist in an interdenominational seminary is to say that I am a missionary focusing on relationships, one whose desire is to make friends with others as part and parcel of my friendship with God. Whenever we can, we must cross the divide between Anabaptists and others to join in the mission of God, testifying that the power of the Spirit creates out of many persons one people who together witness to the One Triune God. And when we cannot cross that divide, when in good conscience we must part ways, we can do so by drawing strength from the best of our Anabaptist sensibilities—by speaking and acting truthfully while seeking to bless those with whom we disagree.

Erin Dufault-Hunter teaches Christian Ethics at Fuller Theological Seminary. She is a long-time member of Pasadena Mennonite Church, where she regularly leads singing and occasionally preaches and teaches.

Anabaptism means visible, "incarnational" witness

Sunoko Lin

Sunoko Lin and family

In 2006, Dave and Rebekka Stutzman moved to California to pursue seminary studies. They soon found a home in a vibrant congregation, Maranatha Christian Fellowship. Part of the Pacific Southwest Mennonite Conference, Maranatha is a church in transition from a first-generation immigrant church to a multicultural church. For several years, Dave and Rebekka have been involved in youth ministry and have worked closely with Maranatha's pastor, Sunoko Lin. The following conversation between Dave and Pastor Sunoko is a snapshot into Maranatha's life and ministry in the San Fernando Valley.

Q. Tell me about the founding story of Maranatha.

A. This church is actually the first church in the San Fernando Valley serving the Indonesian community. It came into existence in 1987 to meet the needs of Indonesian immigrants, particularly Indonesian students at California State University Northridge (CSUN). The composition of the church has, however, changed drastically. Now, most of the people attending are Indonesian immigrant couples with children.

Q. What is the ministry context like in the San Fernando Valley?

A. Our community of San Fernando Valley is an urbanized valley located in the northern section of the city of Los Angeles. It has experienced a tremendous shift in three decades from a predominantly white population to a multiethnic population. The Valley is now home to immigrants from diverse places such as Mexico, El Salvador, Iran, Israel, Armenia, Vietnam, Korea, India and China. One-third of the Valley's 1.7 million residents are foreign born.

Furthermore, our church is located in one of the four poorest communities. Many high-school students do not finish their schooling. Sometimes, you can find three or four families living in one apartment. I have told our church that we need to be aware of these realities in our community. Most of our children in the church are straight "A" students. One of them was even featured in the *Los Angeles Times* for her hard work. So our church has these blessings, and our community has these needs. And so the question is, how can we become a visible witness in this place?

In our church, we are confronted with the transience of our members. People are working labor jobs, in factories, and as waitresses. So there is a high turnover in our church and in all immigrant churches. Most of the immigrants coming to our church are new immigrants from Indonesia. They are in search of a better life with good jobs, better pay, and more opportunities for their children. That is why if they get an opportunity for more affordable living, they will move.

Q. How is the church responding to these challenges?

A. We have discovered that we have a strong community inside the church. When someone has a need, we do not hesitate to help. Hospitality is very important. Indonesians are known for hospitality. That is why we have a meal at every service. Hospitality builds oneness in the church and offers something to others.

Also, our youth ministry has experienced very exciting growth. The youth have brought new life to our first-generation immigrant church. They have helped us see the potential of growing beyond our ethnicity. We are currently studying together how we can effectively transition our church forward. Soon, we will begin offering a combined English and Indonesian service every third week of the month.

> The youth have brought new life to our first-generation immigrant church.

We also want to actively engage the nearby community of Cal State Northridge (CSUN). The campus hosts 31,000 students, making CSUN one of the biggest stakeholders in our community. Its student body presents rich diversity and has students coming from more than 70 different countries. Our location presents us with a wonderful opportunity for global mission. We view CSUN as the spiritual gateway for international outreach. We believe God placed us here for a purpose to be his ambassadors to these students.

Q. What are some of your hopes for the church's ministry?

A. We sense that God is challenging us to dream more about the possible fruits that our church can bear as a faith community. We dream that no one in our church has to go through a painful journey alone, and that the bond that we have should make us ready to journey together in tough times. We dream that we will grow deeper in fellowship in the word of God and prayer, and that we will discover the different spiritual gifts God has given each one of us.

As pastor, it is my prayer that these gifts will be put toward service in the neighboring community. Christian community is above all about service. Christ's love is never inwardly focused, but always outwardly focused. So it is our dream that Maranatha will be recognized as a church where every believer is a minister and that our ministries can bring blessings to others. We hope that our church will have an influence not only inside the church, but also outside our church's wall and be a place where families with hurts will find a place of comfort and healing. Families struggling with parenting can find support and care. Individuals struggling with spiritual and emotional loss will come to us knowing that they will receive support and not judgment.

> One thing that attracted me to Anabaptism, with its emphasis on discipleship and radical faith, is visible witness.

Q. How does Anabaptism shape your view of ministry?

A. One thing that attracted me to Anabaptism, with its emphasis on discipleship and radical faith, is visible witness. For our church in the San Fernando Valley, we must live incarnationally in our community. The church should have an important role in shaping and influencing the life of the community. And for me that is the incarnational message. Anabaptism reminds me that we are to bear fruit. In John 15:1-11 the words "abide in me" appear four times and they mean more than just an imitation of Christ's life and teaching. They point to our active engagement with the One who lives in us by the Holy Spirit. Christ is telling us that fruit-bearing is inevitable when we are connected to him. We need to work with Christ in our engagement with our community. May God's pruning hands be at work in our lives so that we can bear much fruit and be a visible witness!

Sunoko Lin lives with his wife, Natalie, and their three children, Hannah, Daniel and Joshua, in Lake Balboa, Calif. He and his family love traveling, especially summer driving trips. Sunoko is a bivocational pastor. He works as a financial controller while serving at Maranatha Christian Fellowship, a member congregation in Pacific Southwest Mennonite Conference. Sunoko also serves as a board member of Mennonite Mission Network.

But then there was Jesus

Jason Evans

Jason Evans and his family

On an early weekday morning in late 2001, I sat next to my 9-month-pregnant wife, watching a plane crash into the second of the Twin Towers on TV. My arm was wrapped around her. I could feel her belly, stretched tight with our child inside, against my hand. "What kind of world are we bringing this child into?" was all that she could say to me. I had no response.

For weeks, months, the world cast blame on religious radicals for these terrible acts. I found myself asking, "What does my faith have to say about violence?" I am a Christian. I took Church History at a Christian high school. I knew what the church had to say about violence. We embraced it. We became it. I didn't like that. No more than you like reading it. But it was true—the crusades, inquisitions, slavery, and so on. As a political, social and cultural force, the church was often found at the center of some of the most horrific moments in history.

But then there was Jesus. While public Christian figures cast judgment on prime-time television, I found myself reading the Gospels. And there, I could see nothing resembling their rhetoric in Jesus. Jesus blessed peacemakers. He chastised his close friend, Peter, for attacking an officer. He was tortured and sentenced to capital punishment, yet refused to retaliate. Jesus embodied the very opposite of violence. Why was it that we no longer resembled the One who we claimed to follow?

It is one thing to value "community" and "mission" … and quite another to *become* them

In my journey of answering this question, I found myself planting a church that was more a community than congregation. We realized that many of the power and authority structures to which we had become accustomed allowed for a subtle form of violence against lay people. So we decided to do our best to shape a community that functioned more like a spiritual co-operative where we all shared in being a "royal priesthood" rather than having a "professional" carry most of that load. Since we didn't have overhead, we were able to use our resources to take care of each other and others as we discerned together the best way to use our gifts. We met in a home and hosted dialogues rather than sermons. It has not been easy to develop this kind of community, but it has been more than worth it.

> We feel that we have chosen to enter into a stream that has brought back life to our faith.

Along the way, we began to read Anabaptist theologians such as John Howard Yoder and others. Within the Anabaptist stream of Christianity we found a theology that affirmed our convictions. This stream of history felt as though it were ours. Anabaptism drew Christian theology away from a monologue and into dialogue. It became a counterpart in a conversation. And it was always asking, "Yes, we *believe* that, but how do we *live* it?"

To respond to that challenge, we had to look again at how we practiced our faith through the lens of Scripture. Rather than just valuing ideals such as "community" or "mission," could we actually *become* those things together? It has not been easy. We haven't achieved all that we hope to and probably never will. But we feel that we have chosen to enter into a stream that has brought back life to our faith.

Beyond "surviving" to "thriving" as an Anabaptist faith community

As an "outsider" to the Anabaptist tradition, it has often been hard to find a place within the church's institutions. Yet as the church in North America looks to the future with concerns about sustainability, it seems important for us to find ways to learn from each other. The early Anabaptists were sometimes called "the swarm." They were an unstoppable movement that spread across Europe. They found a way to thrive without the weighty demands of the other traditions that hunted them down.

Creative ways to not simply sustain but to thrive are often found at the margins. It never comes easy and most often requires significant sacrifice. As Anabaptists, we have within us the DNA to sustain hard times. I am convinced that some of us as Christian immigrants to Anabaptism are rediscovering many of those ancient ways. And as we do, perhaps our discoveries can be of value to the broader Anabaptist faith community as we together seek how to both survive and thrive in the years ahead.

Jason Evans lives in San Diego, Calif. He has been married to Brooke for 15 years. They have three children, Paige, Matt and Sam. He is the founder of the Ecclesia Collective, a network of grassroots, missional communities.

Anabaptists are well-positioned for making disciples of Jesus
Angela Williams

Angela
Williams

If you ask pastors from virtually any church or denominational background what is central to Christianity, most would claim that discipleship is core to the faith. No true Christian wants to talk about faith void of discipleship. What many church leaders disagree on, however, is how best to cultivate discipleship. How do we actually get there?

I have worked as an intern or on staff in several kinds of churches, Baptist, Foursquare, nondenominational, Presbyterian and Mennonite. Each church has desired to make disciples. And each one has done some significant work, while still missing the mark along the way. That is to be expected; no church performs perfectly. However, there is a common thread in "missing the mark" that should be addressed. While each church wanted the central focus to be discipleship, their primary energies were, in reality, given to something else—creative arts, social justice, entertainment-style worship, "kaleidoscope" theology, or peacemaking, to name a few.

Focus on programs or ideas can hijack the work of disciple-making
This generally happens because the way to make disciples—the ideas or programs that people agree on—became more important than *actually making* the disciples. In the Baptist congregation where I worked, it was about how creative and cool the arts could be. In the Foursquare church, the focal point became social justice—stopping homelessness and feeding people. In the nondenominational setting, the central

focus was more on entertainment, videos, lights and sound. For the Presbyterians, it became making people comfortable and providing a wide spectrum of theology, so that no one felt left out. The tendency in many Mennonite circles is to make protecting heritage or cultivating peace the central focus.

The fact is, discipleship in each of these churches became something that people felt would organically or naturally happen as the ideas or programs were implemented. But when programs or ideas replace the intentional focus on people actually becoming disciples, then disciple-making rarely happens.

Each of the points of emphases I have highlighted is good in and of itself. There should be more attention given to the arts in the life of the church. Social justice is indeed commanded throughout the Bible. It is important to want to reach people visually in a world that presently learns best through this medium. It is pertinent that we allow the gospel to shape people, rather than expecting people to come into our buildings already changed. And the heritage of Mennonites is indeed extremely important, and pacifism is the way of Jesus.

Discipleship should be the main objective, the means and the ends

All of these things are, however, a means to an end. Discipleship should always be the main objective, the means and the ends. Yet, if discipleship is *everything* we do, it usually turns out to receive no attention at all. Disciple-making needs intentionality, its own time, money and people working toward that end. It needs faith communities that understand how one develops into a disciple, and how one nurtures the belief that Jesus was who he said he was, Christ, the son of the living God.

Discipleship starts with and persists in the ongoing work of proclaiming faith in the person of Jesus. Our present postmodern culture resonates most deeply with narrative and storytelling. Discipleship, then, should begin by sharing faith stories. This will not only engage people in a non-alienating way, but will also point them toward faith—the very starting point for discipleship. Sharing our stories of faith should include not only how we originally came to faith, but also how God has consistently met us in our faith journey along the way. Then, there should be a movement from story-sharing to inviting people to experience this

> When programs or ideas replace the intentional focus on people actually becoming disciples, then disciple-making rarely happens.

faith in their own lives. Invitation and intentionality are powerful forces when the two come together. Disciple-making means challenging people to orientate their lives toward the way of Jesus. This involves a first act of putting one's faith in the person of Jesus and accepting who he said he was, and then having faith that the Holy Spirit will assist us as new disciples by working in our lives to make us righteous (Galatians 5:5). In short, the goals of disciple-making are to help people:

- **Know Jesus** (by sharing faith stories).
- **Love Jesus** (by inviting them to have faith).
- **Trust Jesus** (by allowing the Holy Spirit to orientate their lives toward him).

Anabaptists have a special gift to share in disciple-making

This may look different in various contexts, but it is something we undertake in community. Without community, discipleship just becomes another form of therapeutic individualism or mass consumerism. This is why Anabaptism has such an important contribution to make. Anabaptists have a strong connection to one another and have often been a powerful display of community to the world. Anabaptists are committed to living simply and caring about others, pointing beyond self-improvement and satisfied consumerism to the way of Jesus, who calls us to die to self for the sake of our neighbors and the world.

> Disciple-making means challenging people to orientate their lives toward the way of Jesus.

This combination of pacifism and community is what the world is hungry and waiting for. Both Christians and non-Christians alike in this postmodern age are looking for a community that is vibrant and developing rather than stagnant, a story that shows how life with God can be both meaningful and full of passionate possibilities. Mennonites have these things to offer, a lived faith and a firm commitment—not to a set of rules and beliefs—but to the life-giving conviction that one can truly know Jesus by being like him.

If, however, we continue to see our heritage as the "quiet in the land," we will fail in fulfilling Jesus' command to us. Jesus has asked us to *make disciples*. That should make us passionate about inviting people to walk with us toward Jesus. As D.T. Niles has suggested, it is about assisting other beggars to know where to find the bread of life.

I am convinced that if our central concern is actually cultivating disciples of Jesus, in our unique Anabaptist approach and point of view, we will not simply be increasing the ranks of Mennonite adherents, but angels will be rejoicing in heaven because more sinners—just like us—will have come to know new life in Christ and will have joined his disciple band.

Angela Williams is a PhD student in Practical Theology at Fuller Theological Seminary. She enjoys Texas football, Kentucky basketball, working out, and being outdoors. She is currently the director of Youth and Children at Pasadena Mennonite Church.

Anabaptism in a globalized environment
Juan Francisco Martínez

Being an Anabaptist professor at Fuller Seminary provides me with opportunities for unique interactions with students. Some of my students are "cradle" Mennonites who want to understand what it means to be an Anabaptist outside of the Mennonite enclaves of their upbringing. But there are also many young evangelicals from various parts of the world who are looking for deeper expressions of their faith, and who have learned about Anabaptism from friends or by reading people like Hauerwas or Yoder, and are now interacting with Anabaptist professors at this evangelical seminary. These interactions are happening in greater Los Angeles, the boomtown of the Pacific Rim, where the few Mennonite churches in the area are much more likely to have members from Nigeria, Indonesia, Korea or El Salvador than from Pennsylvania, Indiana or Kansas.

Juan Francisco Martínez

What can we learn from newer Anabaptist voices?
What can Mennonites in the rest of the United States learn from the stories of these "new" Anabaptists who are living out a radical discipleship in an urban, multicultural environment far removed from the traditional places where Mennonite identity was formed in the 20th century? The testimonies you just read do not answer the question directly, but they do raise important issues about how Anabaptism can be expressed in a globalized environment.

Several of the storytellers first encountered Anabaptism as a theological ideal in books by Anabaptist theologians. These books described a powerful expression of faith and discipleship. But their encounter with real-life Mennonites has shown them that it is not easy to live out what the authors described. This gets more complicated as people who come from different cultural and national backgrounds interact with U.S. Mennonites, most of whom share a common ethno-religious identity.

While there have been Mennonites of non-European descent in the United States for several generations already, many people in this country closely identify Anabaptism with the Germanic sub-cultures of Mennonitism. More recent waves of Anabaptists are, however, developing models of a faithful church in new cultural situations, even as many are both adapting to U.S. culture and to intercultural life. Here are stories of people who are searching for new ways to be faithful Christians in the midst of rapid and disruptive change. What can they offer U.S. Mennonites, many of whom are also struggling with how to follow Jesus in the midst of the disruptive changes happening in our country?

Stories challenge us to rethink how radical discipleship, ecclesiology, and mission are being lived out in the 21st-century United States.

The stories also challenge us to rethink how radical discipleship, ecclesiology, and mission are being lived out in the 21st-century United States. Though all of those who told their stories are linked to Anabaptist/Mennonite denominations, it is clear that they are pushing beyond the traditional categories of these affiliations. Some contributors are drawing their models of church and community as much from the 16th century as from current Mennonite practices. Might they be pushing us to recognize that 21st-century Anabaptist expressions of church will look more like the untidiness of the 16th century, rather than contained primarily in the U.S. denominational frameworks of the 20th century?

Because of the cultural differences between these new Anabaptists and "ethnic" Mennonites, these stories also invite us to reflect on where the experiences of these two groups intersect and diverge. For example:

- What parts of the 16th-century experience will be considered normative as we revisit the role of the Holy Spirit in the life of the church?
- How does each of these communities understand what it means to follow Jesus when we live in the United States—the last Protestant remnant of Christendom and the principal imperial power in the world today?
- How do the concepts of following Jesus, forming community, nonviolence, and holistic mission look different if one is a Korean

immigrant in Los Angeles as opposed to a Swiss-German Mennonite in Lancaster County?

- How does a middle-class Mennonite invite a poor urban immigrant to a simple lifestyle?
- How do we speak together when the issues each considers crucial at the moment are so different?
- Where and how do we shape the conversations that allow us to address these questions together?

Will Los Angeles be one of the new Anabaptist centers in the 21st century?

Interestingly for me, it seems like southern California is becoming one of those places where some of these conversations might take place. Will southern California be *an* important center of Anabaptist recruitment and expression for the 21st century? What other places exist or can be developed where we can listen to this very diverse, but very committed, new generation of Anabaptists?

These testimonies reflect the joys, the struggles, and the excitement of following Jesus in this complex space that is Los Angeles. My sense is that the future of a global, urban, multicultural Anabaptist understanding of church and mission is in the hands of people like those new Anabaptists who shared their stories and the young "old" Mennonites who helped organize this conversation.

Personally, I was glad to be given the opportunity to join them and to reflect on the experience in this way. This interaction helped me reaffirm my belief in God's future, and called me anew to participate in what God is doing in the world. Listening to the Anabaptist story in places like Los Angeles is a great place to begin thinking about Anabaptist expressions and models of church for our context today. In fact, it challenges us "old" Mennonites to discover the importance of retelling our story in the 21st century.

Juan Francisco Martínez currently lives in Sunland, Calif., where he is married to Olga. He is an associate provost and director of the Hispanic Center at Fuller Seminary where he teaches Anabaptist Theology and Polity. Juan and Olga are part of Iglesia del Pacto in Eagle Rock. Juan enjoys whittling, blogging in Spanish, preaching, reading science fiction, and watching movies with Olga.

Questions for reflection and discussion

1. What comments or insights most struck you in reading this booklet?

2. What are your personal experiences with "new" Anabaptist voices? Are they primarily from non-Germanic communities? From other Christian traditions? First time adherents to the Christian faith?

3. What does it mean to be Anabaptist and multicultural? Anabaptist and urban? Anabaptist and evangelical/charismatic? Are these terms compatible with your understanding of Anabaptist values and perspectives? How might these newer conversations and encounters change the nature of the Mennonite faith family in the U.S. context?

4. Do you have friends—either Christian or non-Christian—who disagree with your Anabaptist perspective? How can you sustain these relationships so that they both sharpen your faithfulness and foster humility?

5. How is the mission of God affected when we isolate ourselves from other Christian brothers and sisters? In what ways can we highlight our shared passion for Scripture, for discipleship, and for the multifaceted mission of Christ and the church?

6. How can Mennonite/Anabaptist faith communities be creative in engaging young people who are less and less compelled by present Christian options?

7. How can our church life and worship be shaped to be more open to non-believers or to those who know nothing about church, "Mennonitism," or even the life of Jesus? Do we truly want to invite more people to faith in Christ, or are we just trying to preserve a cultural heritage?

8. What are we doing in our congregations today that will help the church not only survive but thrive in tomorrow's world?

For further reading

- GORNIK, Mark R., *Word Made Global: Stories of African Christianity in New York City* (Grand Rapids, MI: Eerdmans, 2011).

- HANCILES, Jehu J., *Beyond Christendom: Globalization, African Migration, and the Transformation of the West* (Maryknoll, NY: Orbis, 2008).

- KANAGY, Conrad, *Road Signs for the Journey: A Profile of Mennonite Church USA* (Scottdale, PA: Herald Press, 2007).

- KRABILL, James R. and Stuart MURRAY, *Forming Christian Habits in Post-Christendom* (Elkhart, IN: Institute of Mennonite Studies, 2011).

- MURRAY, Stuart, *The Naked Anabaptist* (Scottdale, PA: Herald Press, 2010).

- POHL, Christine, *Making Room* (Grand Rapids, MI: Eerdmans, 1999).

- SHENK, Joanna, ed., *Extending the Circle: Experiments in Christian Discipleship* (Harrisonburg, VA: Herald Press, 2011).

- SHENK, Wilbert R., *By Faith They Went Out* (Elkhart, IN: Institute of Mennonite Biblical Studies, 2000).

- STONE, Bryan, *Evangelism after Christendom* (Grand Rapids, MI: Brazos Press, 2007).

- WRIGHT, Jeff, *Urban and Anabaptist: The Remarkable Story of Rapid Growth among Mennonites in Southern California,* [in the *Mission Insight* series, No. 22, edited by James R. Krabill] (Elkhart, IN: Mennonite Board of Missions, 2001).

- WRIGHT, Jeff, "Teaching Position or Conversation Starter? *The Confession of Faith in a Mennonite Perspective* and the New Mennonites of Southern California," in *Mennonite Quarterly Review* 81 (3) 2007:427-441.

- YODER, John Howard, *As You Go: The Old Mission in a New Day* [in the *Focal Pamphlet Series,* No. 5] (Scottdale, PA: Herald Press, 1961).